Tahnee and the Peacock Spider

A TALE OF CREATIVITY

STORY BY **ANGELA CASTILLO**
ILLUSTRATED BY **CHER JIANG**
CONTRIBUTOR **HAIYING WU**

No part of this publication may be produced in whole or in part, or stored in a retrieval system, or transmitted in any form, or by any means, electronic, mechanical, photocopying, recording, or otherwise, without written permission of the author.

Text Copyright 2022 Angela Castillo
Illustrations Copyright 2022 Cher Jiang

All Rights Reserved. Published by Angela Castillo
Fayette Press, 1106 Main Street #1471, Bastrop, TX 78602

ISBN: 978-1-953419-59-0 (Softcover)
978-1-953419-60-6 (Hardcover)

To my daughter, Celise.
May you always stay true to your creative heart.

Tahnee added one more dab of paint to her canvas. "What do you think, Peacock Spider?"

"How beautiful!" Peacock Spider waved his front feet. "Did you use every color in your paintbox?"

Tahnee nodded. "I made colors I didn't even know about!"

She glanced down. "Your flowers are lovely. They look so real, like I could almost pick them off the picture."

The two friends stood beside a little pond, surrounded by paperbrush trees. They often came here to paint.

Peacock Spider washed his front legs, which he used for brushes. "I'm finished for today."

Tahnee giggled. "I think you have more paint on you than your canvas!"

Peacock Spider looked at his reflection in the pond. "Silly Tahnee! You know these colors are part of me, not paint."

Tahnee and Peacock Spider packed up their canvases.

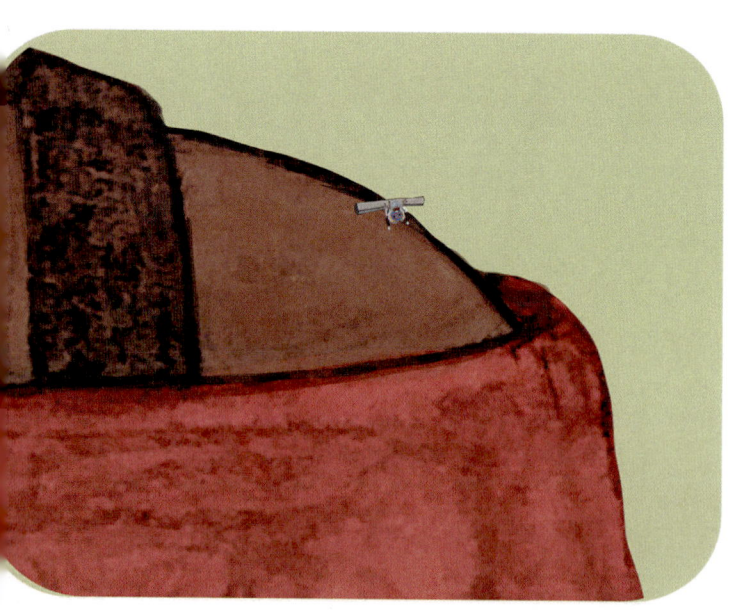

Peacock Spider crawled up Tahnee's shoulder, and they began to walk home.

Frilled-Neck Lizard scurried up to them. "Tahnee! Peacock Spider! Are you going to paint pictures?"

"We already did," said Tahnee, unrolling her painting and spreading it out.

"That's nice, I suppose." Frilled-Neck Lizard blinked. "Why don't you paint a tree branch?"

"Why a tree branch?" asked Peacock Spider.

"I love trees, they are my home," said Frilled-Neck Lizard. "You should only paint tree branches from now on." With that, he scampered off.

Next on the path came Bilby. "Good evening, Peacock Spider and Tahnee!" He sniffed the air. "I smell paint. Did you paint pictures today?"

"Yes," said Peacock Spider.

"Paint the moon for me!" said Bilby. "Every night the moon guides me through the forest. It's my favorite thing."

"Hmmm," said Tahnee.

"You should only paint the moon from now on." Bilby hopped away.

"Silly Bilby," said Peacock Spider, as Tahnee continued home.

Cassowary and Echidna stood in the trail, feathers and fur bristling.

"I was here first!" Echidna shouted.

"No, me," said Cassowary.

They both turned their heads as Peacock Spider and Tahnee approached.

"Hello," said Tahnee.

"Hello." Cassowary stared at her. "You've been painting! I know what you should paint. Kiwi fruits! Lots and lots of kiwi fruits because they are my favorite food."

"No, you should paint ants," said Echidna. "I love to eat yummy, scrumptious ants!"

"Paint kwis!" Cassowary squawked.

"Ants!" Echidna squeaked.

Tahnee walked away, while the two animals continued to argue.

"What should we do?" Tahnee frowned. "I don't want to hurt anyone's feelings, but I don't like painting those things. I paint what I want to paint."

The next day, Cassowary, Echidna, Frilled-Neck Lizard and Bilby gathered in the woods.

"Did Peacock Spider tell you to come to the giant wall?" asked Bilby.

"Yes! I think they painted me a tree branch." Frilled-Neck Lizard hopped up and down.

"No, they painted kiwis!" said Cassowary.

"ANTS!" shouted Echidna, standing on his tiptoes.

Tahnee came into the clearing, her cheeks glowing. "Everyone can come see our painting now."

The animals gasped as they gazed at the picture, created with washable chalk paint.

"It's us, it's us!" shouted Bilby.

"And look at all the beautiful colors!" said Frilled-Neck Lizard. "I do love colors."

"It's the best picture ever." Cassowary wiped away a tear.

"See," Peacock Spider whispered to Tahnee. "The most important thing about art is to express yourself. When you share who you really are, other people will enjoy it, too."

"I'm glad we painted the way we wanted to," said Tahnee.

"So am I," said Peacock Spider.

Animal Facts

Numbat

Though once common in Australia, numbats are now considered endangered, with only 1000 known animals existing.

Considered a marsupial even though they do not possess pouches.

Flying Fox

The largest flying mammal in the world with a wingspan of up to six feet!

Unlike most bats, flying foxes use sight and not echolocation to fly.

Frilled-Neck Lizard

Adult males can reach up to 3 feet in length.

Prefer to spend most of their time in trees, only coming to the ground when food is scarce. They are omnivores and will eat whatever they can.

Peacock Spider

Peacock spiders don't have webs, they prefer to catch their prey by sneaking up on them and pouncing.

Currently, there have been 87 named species of peacock spiders, and more are being discovered on a regular basis.

Cassowary

A cassowary can leap up to 1.5 meters straight up off the ground.

The cassowary is the second-heaviest flightless bird besides the ostrich, even heavier than the emu.

Sugar Glider

Sugar gliders always live in groups which consist of up to seven adults and their babies.

Can float in the air for a distance up to the length of a football field.

Echidna

One of the only mammals that lays eggs but gives milk to its young.

A baby echidna is called a 'puggle.'

Rabbit-Eared Bandicoot

Bandicoots, or 'bilbies,' as they are sometimes called, dig funnel-like holes while searching for insects and plants to eat.

They are marsupials with pouches, but their pouches are backwards to prevent dirt from coming into them while they are burrowing.

Find more of Angela's books, including her books for kids, on Amazon at

Find fun, free activities and more at
http://tobythetrilby.weebly.com

www.amazon.com/Angela-Castillo/e/B00CJUELT0